Taxi Drivers Joke Book

A Bumper Collection of Taxi Driver Jokes

Published by Glowworm Press
7 Nuffield Way
Abingdon OX14 1RL
By Chester Croker

Taxi Driver Jokes

These jokes for taxi drivers will make you giggle. Some of these jokes are old, some are new and we hope you enjoy this bumper collection of the very best taxi drivers jokes and puns around.

This mixture of funny taxi driver jokes will prove that cab drivers do have a good sense of humor. These taxi driver jokes are guaranteed to drive you around the bend and make you laugh out loud.

FOREWORD

When I was asked to write a foreword to this book I was chuffed.

That is until I was told that I was the last resort by the author, Chester Croker, and that everyone else he had approached had said they couldn't do it!

I will give him a *brake* though, as he *wipes me out* with his gags, and I often end up *exhausted* with laughter.

I have known Chester for a number of years and his ability to create funny jokes is absolutely incredible. He is quick witted and an expert at crafting amusing puns.

He will be glad you have bought this book, as he has an expensive lifestyle to maintain.

Enjoy!

Jack Hammer

Table of Contents

Chapter 1: Taxi Drivers Jokes

If you're looking for funny taxi drivers jokes you've certainly come to the right place.

In this book you will find plenty of funny taxi driver jokes that will hopefully make you laugh. Some of these taxi drivers jokes are old, some of them are new, and some will just drive you crazy.

We've got some great one liners to start with, plenty of quick fire questions and answer themed gags, some story led jokes and as a bonus some cheesy pick-up lines that cab drivers could use.

This mixture of jokes will prove taxi drivers have a good sense of humor, and they are guaranteed to get you laughing.

Chapter 2: One Liner Taxi Drivers Jokes

The worst thing about being called Spartacus is that someone else always seems to get my taxi.

I bought a black cab; people love it. Everywhere I go in it, people wave at me.

I got called pretty yesterday and it felt good. Actually, the full sentence was "You're a pretty bad taxi driver." but I'm choosing to focus on the positive.

A taxi driver was fired because he didn't fare well.

I got fired from my last taxi driving job.

People didn't appreciate me going the extra mile.

I forgot a bag of groceries in my taxi and it's been driving me bananas.

A taxi driver's wife asked him to pass her lipstick but he passed her a glue stick instead by mistake. She still isn't talking to him.

I didn't like being a taxi driver. I was convinced that people were always talking behind my back.

Did you hear about the cross-eyed taxi driver who got sacked because he couldn't see eye to eye with his passengers.

In the USA, a hospital bed is like a parked taxi with the meter running.

Taxi drivers are the only people who prefer long ways around to shortcuts.

Did you know that some taxis in Germany can only pick up customers on small side streets? It is what is known as Deutschland uber alleys.

I have had a really bad day. First, my ex got run over by a taxi. Then I got fired from my job – as a taxi driver.

A taxi driver friend of mine gave me some great advice, saying I should put something away for a rainy day.

I've gone for an umbrella.

The foreign guy driving me was really uninspiring and lacking any purpose. He kept saying to me "Give me direction."

Did you hear about the taxi driver who stole a calendar? He got twelve months.

A taxi driver wanted to buy something memorable for his boss, so he bought him a new chair. His boss won't let him plug it in though.

My wife had her taxi driving test last week.

She got eight out of ten.

The other two guys jumped clear.

I am going to set up a taxi company and only employ goofy, lovable, daft, foolish drivers. I am going to call the company Goober.

I saw this odd Bollywood spy movie on the plane the other day. It featured a taxi driver, who was an undercover agent. His catchphrase was "The name's Shaw; Rick Shaw."

I have all the qualifications for being a taxi driver in New York City. I can't speak English and I can't drive.

One time I went for a drive in cinema in a taxi cab.

The movie ended up costing me 85 dollars.

Chapter 3: Q&A Taxi Driver Jokes

Q: What did the taxi driver say to the wolf?

A: *Where-wolf?*

Q: Why did the taxi driver sue the man who died in his cab?

A: *Because life isn't fare.*

Q: How many taxi drivers does it take to change a light bulb?

A: *Two. One to screw it in and one to tell you a story all about changing lightbulbs.*

Q: What's worse for traffic than when it's foggy?

A: *When it's hailing taxis.*

Q: Why do hairdressers make great taxi drivers?

A: *Because they know all the best short cuts.*

Q: Who earns a living driving their customers away?

A: *A taxi driver.*

Q: How do you know when you are drunk?

A: When you get into a taxi cab and you think the fare is the time.

Q: What do you call a man with a shot of whisky on his head?

A: *A taxi. Clearly, he's had too much to drink.*

Q: Why do FBI agents make great cab drivers?

A: *Because when you get in the cab, they already know your name and address.*

Q: What do you call a taxi driver who is happy every single Monday?

A: *Retired.*

Q: What do some women and taxis have in common?

A: *They both make a lot of noise to let you know they are coming.*

Q: What do you call a nun driving a taxi?

A: *Virgin mobile.*

Q: What is Darth Vader's corrupt brother's name?

A: *Taxi Vader.*

Q: Why didn't Hitler take a taxi?

A: *He was more of an Ubermensch.*

Q: Why couldn't the duck billed platypus pay the taxi driver's fare?

A: *He only had one bill.*

Q: What's worse than it raining cats and dogs?

A: *Hailing taxi cabs.*

Q: What do you call a cab which provides drug therapy?

A: *Chemo taxis.*

Q: Why did the cannibal taxi driver get disciplined by his boss?

A: *For buttering up his passengers.*

Q: How do you know when fuel prices are at their highest?

A: *Taxi drivers start to take the shortest route.*

Q: What is a taxi driver's favorite vegetable?

A: *Cab – bage.*

Q: Why do cab drivers expect to be tipped?

A: *Because they think it's fare.*

Chapter 4: Short Taxi Driver Jokes

Guy to Barmaid "Please call me a taxi."

Barmaid "OK - you're a taxi!"

My pal painted his cab yellow on one side and blue on the other.

He reckons that if he was to ever get into an accident, any witnesses are going to contradict one another.

I was a passenger in a cab today, and the jovial driver was whistling and smiling away.

He told me, "I love my job - I'm my own boss, nobody tells me what to do."

I then said, "Take a right turn here."

I was in London today and jumped into the back of a black cab and said to the driver, "Waterloo, please."

He asked, "The station?"

I replied, "Well, I'm a bit late for the battle."

Last night I went to a party. I had quite a few beers, as well as a lot of shots, and then some vodka, a lot of Jagerbombs, and then some more beers.

I was stumbling all over the place, and I realized I was way over the limit so I decided to take a taxi home.

I arrived home safely without incident.

This was a great relief and also a surprise, as I had never driven a taxi before.

A man walks into the casualty department at his local hospital, with his head bleeding.

The nurse asks what happened.

The guy replies, "My wife hit me in the head."

The nurse asks, "Why?"

The guy says, "Well, her parents came over unexpectedly, so my wife she asked me to get them something."

The nurse says, "What did you get them?"

The guy replies, "I got them a taxi."

A taxi driver misjudged a bend and drove his cab into a wall dividing the houses of a Mr. and Mrs. Wilson, and a Mr. and Mrs. Ball.

Mercifully, he was pulled out by the Wilsons.

A drunk was in the back of my cab last night and he asked me if there was enough room in the front for a kebab and a few beers.

I said there was, so he then leant forward and threw up.

A little bird flew into a taxi and was left stunned on the ground.

The taxi driver took pity on the little bird, and took it home and put it into a bird cage.

A little later the bird woke up, looked at its new home, and thought to itself, "Crikey. I must have killed the taxi driver."

A taxi driver is struggling to find a parking spot at the railway station.

"Lord," he prayed. "I can't stand this. If you open a space up for me, I swear I'll give up the booze and go to church every Sunday."

Suddenly, the clouds part and the sun shines down onto an empty parking spot.

Quick as a flash, the taxi driver says: "Never mind Lord, I found one."

A friend of mine had an interview to become a cab driver. He turned up fifteen minutes late for his interview, and the guy interviewing him said straight away "You've got the job."

A taxi driver in my area went to jail for dealing drugs.

I've been one of his customers for well over ten years, and I had no idea that he was a taxi driver.

A taxi driver tries to enter a bar wearing a shirt open at the collar, and is met by a bouncer who tells him that he must wear a necktie to be allowed in.

The resourceful taxi driver goes back to his cab as he knows he has some jump leads in his boot; and he ties these around his neck, with the cable ends dangling free.

He goes back to the bar and the bouncer carefully gives them once over, and then says: "OK, I will let you in - just don't start anything."

A naked woman got into a taxi, and during the journey the cab driver kept staring at her in the mirror.

The woman grew tired of him looking and asked him "Have you not seen a naked woman before?"

He replied, "No madam. I am just curious as to where your money for the fare will come out from."

A taxi driver meets up with his blonde girlfriend as she's picking up her car from the mechanic.

"Everything ok with your car now?" he asks.

"Yes, it's all good," she says.

"Weren't you worried the mechanic might try to rip you off?"

"Yes, but he didn't. I was so relieved when he told me that all I needed was blinker fluid!"

The other day someone jumped into my taxi, pointed to a guy and he demanded, "Follow that guy."

I said, "Sure, what's his Twitter name?"

Scot to Taxi driver: "How much is it to the airport?"

Taxi driver: "It will be sixty pounds."

Scot: "And how much for the luggage?"

Taxi driver: "The luggage is free."

Scot: "In which case, just take my luggage, I'll get the bus."

Son: "Hey Dad, I'm going to the airport. Please call me a taxi."

Father: "OK. Hello taxi."

Two taxi cabs crashed into each other. "What's the matter with you?" shouted one of the drivers, "are you blind?"

"Blind?" said the other driver. "I hit you, didn't I?"

One for the kids:- A cab driver sees two bags of crisps ambling along the side of the road. He stops and asks them if they need a lift. One tells him, "No need - we are both Walkers."

A husband and wife are having an argument when the wife says, "If I hear another word from you I am leaving and I am going to live with my mother."

The husband says, "Taxi."

A dog walks into a pub, and orders a drink saying to the barman, "Can I have a pint of lager and a packet of nuts please."

The barman says, "Wow, that's amazing; you should join the circus."

The dog replies, "Why? Do they need taxi drivers?"

A proud father is showing pictures of his three sons to an old friend and he is asked, "What do your boys do for a living?

He replied, "Well my youngest is a surgeon and my middle is an attorney."

"What does the oldest child do?" his friend asked.

The reply came, "He's the taxi driver that paid for the others' education."

A cab driver was driving recklessly when his passenger could stand no more.

She leaned forward and said, "Would you please slow down and be more careful? I have five children at home."

"Crikey, madam." grumbled the cabbie. "You've got five kids and you're telling me to be careful?"

A taxi driver goes to the doctor with a hearing problem.

The doctor says, "Can you describe the symptoms to me?"

The taxi driver replies, "Yes. Homer is a big fat yellow lazy man and his wife Marge is skinny with big blue hair."

A taxi driver took his cross-eyed dog to the vet.

The vet picked the dog up to examine him and said, "Sorry, I'm going to have to put him down."

The taxi driver said, "It's not that bad is it?"

The vet replied, "No, he's just very heavy."

A taxi driver complained to his friend that his wife doesn't satisfy him anymore.

His friend advised he find another woman on the side, pretty sharpish.

When they met up a month or so later, the taxi driver told his friend, "I took your advice. I managed to find a woman on the side, but my wife still doesn't satisfy me."

A taxi driver had a roofer called Gary working on his house repairing some roof tiles.

Gary is up on the roof and accidentally cuts off his ear, and he yells down to the taxi driver, "Look out for my ear I just cut off."

The taxi driver looks around and calls up to Gary, "Is this your ear?"

Gary looks down and says, "Nope. Mine had a pencil behind it!"

I have had a really bad day today.

First of all, my ex got run over by a taxi.

Then I was sacked from my job - as a taxi driver.

A taxi driver asks his lawyer "How much do you charge?"

"Two hundred and fifty dollars for three questions." the lawyer replies.

"Isn't that rather expensive?" the taxi driver asked.

"Yes," the lawyer replied. "What's your third question?"

So I said to my cab driver, "King Arthur's Close.

He replied, "Don't worry; we'll lose him at the next set of lights."

Chapter 5: Longer Taxi Driver Jokes

The Priest

A priest and a crazy taxi driver die and go to heaven and are welcomed by St. Peter who first of all shows the taxi driver his new home, which is a lavish castle fully equipped with servants.

He then shows the priest his new home which is a tiny hut with no electricity.

The priest asks how this could happen, and St Peter told him, "During your Sunday sermons everybody fell asleep; while every time that crazy taxi driver had passengers in his cab, they all prayed."

Nuclear War

A young taxi driver is sitting at the bar after work one night, when a large sweaty construction worker sits down next to him.

They start talking and eventually the conversation gets on to nuclear war.

The taxi driver asks the construction worker, "If you hear the sirens go off, the missiles are on their way, and you've only got 20 minutes left to live, what will you do?"

The construction worker replies, "I am going to make it with anything that moves."

The construction worker then asks the taxi driver what he would do to which he replies, "I'm going to keep perfectly still."

Street Walkers

A woman and her teenage son were in a taxi when they saw a number of prostitutes standing by the roadside.

The boy asked, "What are all those women doing?"

"They're waiting for their husbands to get off work," his mother replied.

The taxi driver turns around and says, "Geez lady, why don't you tell him the truth? They're hookers- they are women who have sex with men for money."

The little boy's eyes widened and he says, "Is that true Mom?"

His mother, glaring at the driver, answers, "Yes."

The boy then asks, "Mom, if those women have babies, what happens to them?"

His mother replies, scornfully, "Most of them become taxi drivers."

The Pastor

A taxi driver has been driving for many years in his city, and has always followed the law and obeyed traffic light signals. Over the years he has got more and more frustrated with the bad tempered cyclists who do not follow the rules of the road, and act like they can do whatever they like; so every now and again the taxi driver gently bumps into the cyclists accidentally on purpose.

One normal day, a pastor gets in the cab and he asks to go to the other side of city. Almost immediately the taxi is stuck behind a cyclist who is going way too slow for motor traffic and he won't pull to the side.

After ten minutes of frustration, room finally opens up for the driver to pass the cyclist. Even better, it's a great opportunity to knock the selfish cyclist off the road. Just before impact though, the taxi driver remembers his passenger and decides he couldn't do such an evil thing in the company of a pastor.

The taxi driver makes to pass the cyclist very closely, to still scare him when suddenly the pastor swings his door open. The door hits the cyclist hard on the back and he's sent flying off his bike.

The taxi driver is dumbfounded at what happened, but the pastor just smiles, and says, "It's a good thing I was paying attention, you almost missed him!"

Taxi to the Hospital

A woman flagged down a cab and told the driver to take her to the hospital.

"Where at the hospital?" the cabbie asked.

"The maternity ward." the woman answered.

A gritty look came across the cabbie's face and he said, "Don't worry, love – I'll get you there as soon as I can."

He then started driving quite fast, and was weaving past other cars on the road.

"Slow down, there's no emergency," the woman directed. "I work at the hospital – I am a midwife."

The Roses

A couple was going out for the evening. They had gotten ready and were all dolled-up when the taxi arrived.

The taxi arrives and as they don't want the dog shut in, the wife goes out to the taxi while the husband goes to put the dog out into the yard.

The wife, not wanting the cabbie to know that the house will be empty explains to him, "He's just going upstairs to say good-bye to my mother."

A few minutes later, the husband gets into the cab and says, "Sorry I took so long."

He continues, "The stupid bitch was hiding under the bed and I had to poke her with a coat hanger to get her to come out. Then I had to wrap her in a blanket to keep her from scratching and biting me as I hauled her arse downstairs and tossed her out in the back yard. Let's just hope she doesn't sh*t in the roses tonight."

Rabbi Takes A Ride

A rabbi is in a taxi, going into the city for a meeting. Everything is fine, the driver is courteous when whilst they are waiting a traffic lights, a gang of thugs turn up, armed with baseball bats and they start hitting the car, and break the lights, and they get the driver out and kick him a few times.

The rabbi is scared and screams, "Please stop, please... stop it."

Then another gang shows up, and they fight off the first gang and then turn to the taxi and smash up the vehicle. The cab has all its windows broken and the rabbi screams, "Please stop, please... stop it."

The police turn up, and handcuff some of the gang members, call for an ambulance for the driver. Meantime, the rabbi is still in the back of the taxi and seems more and more agitated as he continues to say, "Please stop, please... stop it."

A policeman helps him out, and sees the terror on his face. "Calm down, we saved you, everything is alright," he says.

The rabbi tells him, "Please stop, please... stop it."

The policeman tries to reassure him saying, "Everything is alright, you're safe."

The rabbi looks the policeman in the eye and says, "Please stop, please... stop the meter!"

A Nun's Surprise

A nun gets into a taxi and the driver just can't take his eyes off her.

Eventually, he says, "Sister, I must tell you something but I don't want to offend you."

She says, "My son, you won't offend me. I've heard it all after many years of being a nun."

"Okay," says the cab driver, "Well, I always had this fantasy of kissing a nun."

"I can agree to that my son, but only if you are single and Catholic," says the nun.

The cabbie says, "No problem, I'm both!"

He stops and the nun makes his dreams come true with some very deep kissing.

After they set off again, the driver starts crying and says "I'm sorry Sister," he says. "I have a confession to make. I lied to you; I'm married and I'm Jewish."

"That's alright my son," replied the nun. "My name is Brian and I'm on my way to a fancy dress party."

The Irish Cab Driver

An Irish cab driver backed into a stationary market stall in view of a policeman who just happened to be walking along.

The policeman started his questioning of the cab driver.

"What is your name?"

"Paddy O'Sullivan."

"That's the same as mine. Where are you from?"

"County Donegal."

"That's the same as me."

The policeman paused and said, "Hang on a moment, I think I need to have a few words with the fella that ran into the back of your cab."

Hurry To The Airport

A man is in a taxi on the way to the airport and he said to the driver, "Please hurry up, I really need to get to the airport as fast as possible."

"I'll do my best, sir. Why are you in such a hurry?" replied the driver.

"I am late for the flight, now drive faster please," the passenger said.

"What flight are you on then?" the driver asked.

"RyanAir 424 now please shut up and drive," the passenger angrily replied.

"Worry not, sir. My app here shows that flight 424 will be delayed until further notice." the driver said.

The passenger replied, "Yes that's right – that's because I'm the pilot of that flight."

Becks

David Beckham gets into a taxi and says, "Heathrow Airport please."

During the journey Becks notices the driver giving him a few looks in the mirror.

This happens continuously until they approach the airport when the driver says, "Come on mate; give us a clue?"

Beckham replies, "I had a great career at Manchester United and Real Madrid and I won over 100 England caps."

The cab driver says, "No, you thick idiot, which terminal do you want?"

At The Strip Club

A wife decides to treat her husband on his birthday by taking him to a strip club.

At the club, the doorman says, "Hey Ronnie, how are you tonight?"

The wife asks her husband, "How does he know you?"

Ronnie says, "I play golf with him."

Inside the strip club, the bartender says, "The usual, Ronnie?"

Ronnie says to his wife, "Before you say anything dear, he is on the darts team."

Then a hot stripper sidles up and says, "Hi Ronnie! Good to see you again. Do you want the special again?"

The wife is so angry at this, she storms out of the club dragging Ronnie with her and they both get into a waiting taxi.

The taxi driver says, "Hey Ronnie boy, your standards are slipping – you've picked up a real ugly one tonight!"

Romantic Drive

A guy and a girl are on a first date, and after enjoying a romantic meal, the guy drives her out to the countryside where they park next to a wood, and feeling frisky, they both get into the back seat of the car.

Whilst they were the caressing the woman suddenly pulled back and declared, "I'm sorry about this and I should have told you earlier but I actually do this for a living and if you want to go all the way with me it will cost you 100 dollars."

The cabbie was stunned, but being caught up in the heat of the moment, agreed to her demands.

After the pair have had a good time, they get back into the front seats, when the guy announces, "I'm really sorry about this and I should have told you earlier, but I'm actually a cabbie, and it's going to cost you 100 dollars to get home."

Unlucky

After a few years of married life, a taxi driver finds that he is no longer able to perform.

He goes to his doctor, and he is referred to a psychiatrist.

After a few visits, the shrink confesses, "I am at a loss as to how you could possibly be cured." Finally, the psychiatrist refers him to a witch doctor.

The witch doctor meets with the cab driver and assures him he has a cure. He throws some powder onto a fire and there is a flash with billowing blue smoke.

The witch doctor says, "This is powerful healing, but you can only use it once a year. All you have to do is say '1-2-3' and your member shall rise for as long as you wish."

The witch doctor continues, "All you or your partner has to say is '1-2-3-4' and it will go down. But be warned - it will not work again for a year."

The cabbie goes home and that night, he is ready to surprise his wife with the good news.

He lies in bed with her and says, "1-2-3," and speedily gets an erection.

His wife turns over to him and says, "What did you say '1-2-3' for?"

Three Friends

Ron is talking to two of his friends, Jim and Shamus.

Jim says, "I think my wife is having an affair with a taxi driver. The other day I came home and found a road map under our bed and it wasn't mine."

Shamus then confides, "Well I think my wife is having an affair with an electrician. The other day I found some wire cutters under the bed and they weren't mine."

Ron thinks for a minute and then says, "You know - I think my wife is having an affair with a horse."

Both Jim and Shamus look at him in complete disbelief.

Ron sees them looking at him and says, "No, seriously. The other day I came home early and found a jockey under our bed."

Made In Japan

A Japanese man went to America for sightseeing. On the last day, he hailed a cab and told the driver to drive to the airport. During the journey, a Honda drove past the taxi.

Thereupon, the man leaned out of the window excitedly and yelled, "Honda, very fast. Made in Japan."

After a while, a Toyota sped past the taxi. Again, the Japanese man leaned out of the window and yelled, "Toyota, very fast. Made in Japan."

And then a Mitsubishi sped past the taxi. For the third time, the Japanese leaned out of the window and yelled, "Mitsubishi, very fast. Made in Japan."

When the taxi got to the airport, the fare was recorded as 200 dollars. The Japanese guy exclaimed, "Wah. So expensive."

Immediately the driver bawled back, "Meter, very fast. Made in Japan."

Reunion

A group of cabbies, all aged 40, discussed where they should meet for a reunion lunch. They agreed they would meet at a place called The Dog House because the barmaids had big breasts and wore mini-skirts.

Ten years later, at age 50, the cabbies once again discussed where they should meet for lunch. It was agreed that they would meet at The Dog House because the food and service was good and there was an excellent beer selection.

Ten years later, at age 60, the friends again discussed where they should meet for lunch. It was agreed that they would meet at The Dog House because there was plenty of parking to park their taxis, they could dine in peace and quiet, and it was good value for money.

Ten years later, at age 70, the friends discussed where they should meet for lunch. It was agreed that they would meet at The Dog House because the restaurant was wheelchair accessible and had a toilet for the disabled.

Ten years later, at age 80, the cabbies, now all retired, discussed where they should meet for lunch. Finally it was agreed that they would meet at The Dog House because they had never been there before.

Surprise

Jim grabbed his suitcase off the luggage carousel and headed outside to hail a taxi. A taxi promptly picked him up and they were on their way.

Twenty minutes into the ride Jim had a question for the taxi driver.

"Excuse me sir" said Jim tapping the driver on the shoulder.

"Arghhhhh" screamed the taxi driver, swerving the taxi across a lane of traffic before coming to a halt.

"What was that all about?" demanded Jim.

"I'm sorry," said the taxi driver, wiping his brow, "this is my first day on the job; I've been driving a hearse for the last twenty years!"

Interrogation

A taxi driver was being interrogated after an accident.

Police Officer: "So, how did you kill 19 people?"

Taxi Driver: "I was driving along when I saw two men crossing the road. On the other side, there was a wedding party. I hit the brakes, but they failed."

Police Officer: "Carry on."

Taxi Driver: "I had to quickly make the choice of either hitting the two men, or the wedding party."

Police Officer: "You hit the two men, of course."

Taxi Driver: "Exactly. The problem was, after hitting one of the men, the other man escaped across the road to the wedding party, so I went after him."

The Parrot and the Taxi Driver

A taxi driver is called to pick up an old lady. He goes to the front door, and she greets him saying she won't be long and tells him to wait in the kitchen, where there is a restless drooling Doberman and a contented parrot siting on his perch.

The taxi driver asks the little old lady if he'll be safe while she's getting her things and she smiles and says, "Oh yes! Poopsie is so sweet. He wouldn't hurt a fly. He's a good doggie, but whatever you do, do NOT say anything to the parrot."

Relieved, the taxi driver starts messaging on his phone. However, the parrot starts to call the taxi driver all manner of rude names.

Losing his temper, the taxi driver glares at the bird and screams, "Shut up, you annoying bird."

The parrot is stunned into silence, and a few seconds later, it squawks, "Stick it to him, Poopsie!"

The Frog

An 84 year old retired taxi driver was walking along the road one day when he came across a frog.

He reached down, picked the frog up, and began to put it in his pocket. As he did so, the frog said, "Kiss me on the lips and I'll turn into a beautiful woman and show you a very good time."

The retired taxi driver carried on putting the frog in his pocket.

The frog said, "Didn't you hear what I said?"

The taxi driver looked at the frog and said, "Yes, but at my age I'd rather have a talking frog."

Pulling Power

Carlo the property developer and his taxi driver buddy Doug, went bar-hopping every week together, and every week Carlo would go home with a hot woman while Doug went home alone.

One week Doug asked Carlo his secret to picking up women.

Carlo says, "When you're on the dance floor and she leans in and asks you what you do for a living, don't tell her you're a cabbie. Tell her you're a lawyer."

Later Doug is dancing with a woman when she asks him what he does for a living. "I'm a lawyer," says Doug. The woman smiles and asks, "Want to go back to my place? It's just around the corner."

They go to her place, have some fun and an hour later, Doug is back in the pub telling Carlo about his success.

"I've only been a lawyer for an hour," Doug tittered, "And I've already screwed someone!"

Exact Words

The tired husband was relay pleased that his pre-booked taxi driver had waited five hours at the airport after his flight was delayed.

He said to the cabbie, "Thanks so much for waiting and in order to thank-you, here's an extra 100 dollars to take the missus out to dinner."

Later that night, the doorbell rang and it was the taxi driver.

Thinking the cabbie had forgotten something the man asked, "What's the matter, did you forget something?"

"Nope." replied the taxi driver, "I'm just here to take your missus out to dinner like you asked."

Train Passengers

A taxi driver, a lawyer, a beautiful lady, and an old woman were on a train, sitting 2x2 facing each other.

The train went into a tunnel and when the carriage went completely dark, a loud "thwack" was heard.

When the train came out of the tunnel back into the light the lawyer had a red hand print on his face. He had been slapped on the face.

The old lady thought, "That lawyer must have groped the young lady in the dark and she slapped him."

The hottie thought, "That lawyer must have tried to grope me, got the old lady by mistake, and she slapped him."

The lawyer thought, "That taxi driver must have groped the hottie, she thought it was me, and slapped me."

The taxi driver sat there thinking, "I can't wait for another tunnel so I can slap that lawyer again!"

Three Daughters

A male taxi driver was talking to two of his friends about their teenage daughters.

The first friend says, "I was cleaning my daughter's room the other day and I found a pack of cigarettes. I didn't even know she smoked."

The second friend says, "That's nothing. I was cleaning my daughter's room the other day and I found a half full bottle of Vodka. I didn't even know she drank."

The taxi driver says, "That's nothing. I was cleaning my daughter's room the other day and I found a pack of condoms. I didn't even know she had a penis."

Chapter 6: Taxi Drivers Pick-Up Lines

Want to be my backseat driver?

I can give you a ride anytime, day or night.

I'll let you know when it's time to get off.

Are you going my way?

Do you believe in love at first sight or should I drive by again?

Need a ride?

I will drive you crazy.

You can have as many rides as you want.

I can go as fast or as slow as you like.

I would drive a million miles for one of your smiles.

Chapter 7: Bumper Stickers for Taxi Drivers

I am a taxi driver. What is your super power?

Getting you home safely.

Trust me. I am a taxi driver.

Have you hugged a taxi driver lately?

Taxi drivers make better lovers.

Designated drunkard.

No cash left in this vehicle overnight.

I am not a taxi driver. I am just a girl with a car.

Need a ride?

Don't get hammered. Take a taxi cab.

Chapter 8: Summary

Hey, that's pretty well it for this book. I hope you've enjoyed it.

I've written a few other joke books for other professions, and here are just a few sample jokes; these are from my electricians joke book:-

Q: What kind of van does an electrician drive?

A: A Volts-wagon.

Q: What do you call a Russian electrician?

A: Switchitonanov.

Q: What is the definition of a shock absorber?

A: A careless electrician.

About the Author

Chester Croker has written many joke books and he has twice been voted Comedy Writer Of The Year by the International Jokers Guild.

He is known to his friends as Chester the Jester or Croker the Joker and has spent many hours of his life talking to cab drivers in many countries around the world which has provided him with plenty of material for this joke book.

If you see anything wrong, or you have a gag you would like to see included in the next edition of this book, please let us know via the glowwormpress.com website.

If you did enjoy the book, kindly leave a review on Amazon so that other cab drivers can have a good laugh too.

Thanks in advance.

Printed in Great Britain
by Amazon

54565309R00043